In our classroom

The bags go here.

Jaimen
Sophie
James

The books go here.

The Minister's Ca
ABC
Lynley Dodd
uckat
Gaelyn Gordon
Chris Gaskin
That's how
learn

The pencils go here.

Librar
Corn
Have A Go!
Pencils

The blocks go here.

The letters go here.

September
October
A B C D

The puzzles go here.

four
five
chickens
six
cats
7
8
eight
clocks
9
nine
butterflies
ten
sweets
11
eleven
kites
12
twelve
snakes
13
thirteen
balls
14
fourteen
cakes
15
fifteen
flags
16
sixteen
mice
17
seventeen
strawberries
18
eighteen
ice-creams
19
nineteen
pencils
20
twenty
flag
traffic sign
mirror
brooch
star fruit
12 1 2 3 4 5 6 7

The flowers go here.

Science
Science

The paintings go up here.